DATE DUE

LIFE INSIDE THE
AIR FORCE
ACADEMY

MAGDALENA ALAGNA

HIGH
interest
books

Children's Press®
A Division of Scholastic Inc.
New York/Toronto/London/Auckland/Sydney
Mexico City/New Delhi/Hong Kong
Danbury, Connecticut

Book Design: Dan Hosek
Contributing Editor: M. B. Pitt

Photo Credits: Cover © The Military Picture Library/Corbis; p. 5 © George Hall/
Corbis; pp. 7, 8, 9, 12, 13, 15, 17, 18, 19, 21, 22, 27, 29, 31, 32, 33, 35, 37, 38, 41
courtesy of Defense Visual Information Center, March ARB, California; p. 10
© Richard Hamilton Smith/Corbis; p. 25 © Leif Skoogfors/Corbis

Library of Congress Cataloging-in-Publication Data

Alagna, Magdalena.
Life inside the Air Force Academy / by Magdalena Alagna.
    p. cm. -- (Insider's look)
Includes index.
Summary: Explores the challenges and rewards of attending the Air Force
Academy in Colorado Springs, Colorado, where individuals are trained to
become officers in the United States Air Force.
ISBN 0-516-23924-4 (lib. bdg.) -- ISBN 0-516-24001-3 (pbk.)

1. United States Air Force Academy--Juvenile literature. [1. United
States Air Force Academy. 2. Occupations.] I. Title. II. Series.
UG638.5.P1 A8 2002
358.4'0071'173--dc21
                                                    2002001901

CONTENTS

Introduction

If you've been to an air show, you may know the feeling—an almost giddy rush as you scan the skies. You see several supersonic jets loop and twist. You watch the aircraft perform breathtaking dives. Your jaw drops in awe. The show ends—but your imagination stays in the clouds. Where, you wonder, did the flying aces inside those cockpits learn their skills and get their wings?

There's a great chance they got their start at the United States Air Force Academy. For nearly fifty years, the academy has provided a training ground for our nation's aviators. Pilots who protect the United States come from this institution.

The U.S. Air Force Academy (USAFA) is located in Colorado Springs, Colorado. With its mountainous terrain and wide-open spaces, Colorado Springs is the perfect setting to launch and fly aircraft. Each year, 12,000 men and women apply to the USAFA. Only about 1,300 are selected. Those who do join make more than a commitment to taking classes. They commit to serve their nation's defense after graduation.

How does one apply for the academy? What is the life of an USAFA cadet like? Is USAFA any different from a civilian college? How much military service are cadets expected to provide in return for their education? This book will answer these questions and more.

CHAPTER ONE

Rising Force

HISTORY LESSON

The idea for the academy began taking shape in 1949. A group of educators met to discuss the United States Air Force (USAF). The educators knew that, with each passing year, military aircraft was becoming more sophisticated. It was crucial that pilots received the best training possible. This group believed that the USAF shouldn't have to rely on other military branches for their pilots. They felt strongly that the USAF should have its own academy. This academy would produce its own crop of outstanding officers. The officers would be trained, tested, and ready to patrol the skies in their country's defense.

The USAFA was created so that men and women could be trained with one mission: to secure the skies

One educator present at the meeting was Dwight D. Eisenhower. Eisenhower had been the Supreme Commander of the Allied Forces in World War II. In 1953, Eisenhower became the president of the United States. He didn't forget that important meeting. On April 1, 1954, President Eisenhower signed a bill creating the United States Air Force Academy. The first entering class of 306 men began training on July 11, 1955.

WHAT IS LEARNED

The USAFA mission statement is to inspire and develop outstanding young men and women to become knowledgeable USAF officers who have character and discipline.

The four-year program focuses on more than academics to achieve these standards. It also helps

ACADEMY FACTS

WOMEN TAKE FLIGHT
The biggest change to the academy's enrollment came in October 1975. President Gerald Ford signed a controversial law allowing women into the USAFA. The first female graduates completed their training in May 1980.

students strengthen their bodies as well as their characters. Heavy focus is placed on career development. Students learn to apply their studies to their military careers, and beyond.

Career development is split into four areas. They are professional military studies, leadership skills, aviation science and airmanship programs, and military training. These areas give cadets the knowledge, skills, and values they'll need as officers.

Before they ever fly solo, USAFA cadets are given hundreds of hours of flight training.

Upon graduation, cadets are made second lieu-tenants in the U.S. Air Force!

GETTING IN

To apply for admission to the academy, you must be an unmarried U.S. citizen and you must not have any children depending on you for their survival. On July 1st of the year you're applying, you must be between the ages of seventeen and twenty-two.

The academy breaks down its review process of an applicant into three parts. Each part is scored. Added together, the parts make up each applicant's total score. First, the USAFA selects cadets who

Those who aspire to join the USAFA must excel in high school. Each year, the academy raises the bar on their admission standards.

excelled in high school. Eighty-nine percent of "doolies" (see box below) ranked in the top one-fifth of their high school graduating class. Almost all applicants scored well on the SAT and ACT. These academic factors make up 60 percent of an applicant's score.

Secondly, applicants have to prove that they took part in after-school activities. The selection committee expects to see extracurricular involvement. They are impressed when they see applicants who were leaders of clubs and sports teams. Applicants must also pass a candidate fitness test.

The USAFA classifies their cadets differently than a civilian college.

USAFA DESIGNATION	USAFA NICKNAME	CIVILIAN COLLEGE NAME
Cadet Fourth Class (C4C)	Four degree, or "doolie"	Freshman
Cadet Third Class (C3C)	Three degree	Sophomore
Cadet Second Class (C2C)	Two degree, Non-commisioned officer	Junior
Cadet First Class (C1C)	Firstie, cadet officer	Senior

This test measures how many pull-ups, sit-ups, and push-ups an applicant can do. Cadet hopefuls are also timed on sprints. They must be able to run three 100-yard sprints. Males have 60 seconds to complete all three. Females get 69 seconds. Another 20 percent of the score hinges on this area.

Finally, candidates are evaluated and interviewed by committee members. Each candidate's current record is discussed, as well as his or her potential. An entrance essay is carefully studied. These factors make up the last 20 percent of an applicant's score. Once accepted to the USAFA, your tuition is free. However, you have a lot of work to do in exchange!

ACADEMY FACTS It pays to be a cadet—sort of. Cadets earn $700 per month. However, they only see a little of the money. Checks are deposited directly into a special account. Then, the cadet's expenses are subtracted from the pay. These charges include costs for uniforms, computers, haircuts, and sheets. Cadets also earn $5.45 each day for food. This money is automatically transferred to Mitchell Hall, the academy's dining commons.

The tough admission guidelines make getting into the USAFA an uphill climb.

CHAPTER TWO

Training and Lifestyle

Your first days at the academy are packed with tests and paperwork. You'll fill out administrative forms. You'll take both physical exams and written placement tests. These tests help teachers discover what your abilities are. They also reveal which areas you might need help in.

The lifestyle at most civilian colleges can be pretty laid-back. Many professors don't mind if students come to class wearing worn-out jeans or a wrinkled shirt. Academy life plays by an entirely different set of rules. You must wear a uniform to each class. Not only that, but you're expected to wear military dress during training and all formal events.

A private study session provides a rare occasion for this cadet to wear casual clothing.

You and a roommate will live in one of two dormitories, Vandenberg or Sijan Halls. The two of you are expected to keep your room in top shape. Leaving pizza slices on the bed or dirty laundry in the corner will spell trouble for you.

The huge dining room, Mitchell Hall, serves all cadets at once. In military life, most activities— even leisure time—are done on a timed schedule. For instance, you only have 25 minutes to eat!

Academy days are filled from sunrise to sundown. You'll be packing in classes, military training, study periods, and exams. You'll have one hour for assembly and lunch. In the afternoons, cadets focus on athletics and extracurricular activities. After the evening meal, you must be ready for a hard night of studying.

ACADEMICS

Completed studies lead to a Bachelor of Science degree. The USAFA requires 112 semester hours in core courses. This is a higher load than most civilian colleges demand.

The hours are equally divided between engineering and basic sciences, and humanities and social sciences. Cadets must also take semester hours in other fields. These fields are air force operations, physical education, and military strategic studies. There are thirty-one majors, and 500 classes, to choose from. The most popular majors include management, international affairs and political science, and the many kinds of engineering.

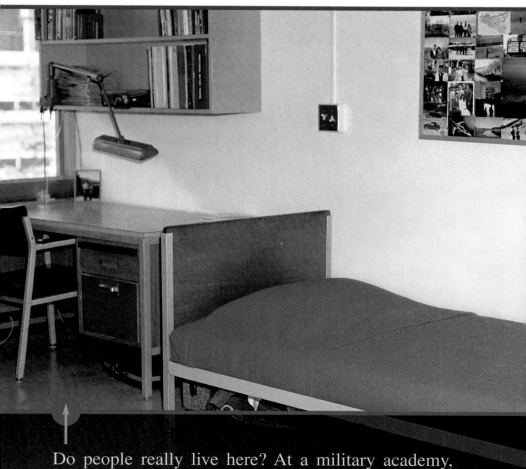

Do people really live here? At a military academy, sloppy dorm rooms are strictly forbidden.

BRIEF BREAKS

Summer breaks at the USAFA are much briefer than those at civilian universities. In fact, some of the most important military training occurs between semesters. Cadets take two, three-week training periods each summer. The other three weeks give cadets a chance to cash in on some well-earned rest!

BASIC CADET TRAINING

Basic Cadet Training (BCT) is a grueling, five-week introduction to military life. All incoming cadets go through BCT the first summer in Colorado. BCT consists of two parts. The first part takes place in the Cadet Area of campus. The second part occurs in Jack's Valley. Jack's Valley is a wooded area located on academy grounds.

ACADEMY FACTS The Honor Code is the centerpiece of cadet life. It demands complete honesty and integrity. Cadets suspected of violating the code go through a process similar to a trial. Violations are investigated. All evidence is reviewed. Cadets found guilty may be severely punished. They can be placed on probation or suspended from the academy.

a crash course for new cadets. While it leaves many cadets nursing aches and pains, it prepares them well for the four years to come.

The first portion of BCT is designed to help new cadets make the transition to military life. They learn the academy's many rules, duties, and expectations. Upper-class cadets teach new cadets the basics in air force customs, courtesies, and history. They also teach younger cadets how to handle and clean a rifle, and how to march. Most importantly, new cadets are introduced to the Air Force Academy Honor Code.

Once in Jack's Valley, cadets' bodies are taxed to the limit. Cadets are expected to show up to BCT in good shape. If they're not, instructors will make sure cadets get in shape in a hurry—and stay that way! The punishing physical activities that cadets endure at Jack's Valley build self-confidence and teamwork.

DOOLIES DO IT ALL

You've made it through basic training! You're officially a doolie. What do you study next? Doolies study the military's role in American society. They also study the air force's mission. Sophomores study communication skills. Juniors study the air force's combat and operational aspects. Seniors study military history and strategy.

The first portion of BCT is designed to drill USAFA traditions and rules into the cadets' heads.

The academy is no place for those with a fear of flying (or falling). As part of their training, cadets learn high-altitude parachuting skills.

Of course, if you're in the USAFA, chances are that you long to operate and fly a plane. The academy offers numerous courses in flying, navigation, and parachuting. You start with basic skills. You also may fly light aircraft with the cadet aviation club. Astronomy and advanced navigation courses are also available.

COMBAT SURVIVAL TRAINING (CST)

Combat Survival Training (CST) is a three-week program. It occurs during the cadets' second summer. Should cadets ever find themselves in the heat of battle, CST prepares them for some of the troubles they would face.

During CST, crucial skills are learned swiftly. For three days, cadets study books about survival. Then they receive two days of on-base survival training. There are eight days of field training and one day of water survival training. Cadets learn how to get a rescue aircraft to disaster survivors. One day is devoted to parachute jumping and landing techniques. Cadets learn how to survive harsh climates and many different types of terrain.

Cadets also take courses that help them understand racial and gender issues. Part of good leadership is being aware of what others are going through. This includes being able to put yourself in the place of someone who is of a different race or gender.

Cadets trek through the Rocky Mountains during CST. While there, they learn survival lessons that are crucial to their military careers. They discover how to build their own shelters and how to get food in hostile environments. They also learn the tactic of evasion. Evasion is the art of avoiding enemy capture while in battle.

For the other second-summer training period, cadets have choices. They can work at an air force base. They can also choose to do airborne or basic parachute training. During their last two summers, cadets are urged to take leadership roles. They often become supervisors or instructors in basic cadet and survival training.

AIRMANSHIP

Airmanship is the study of flying and navigating aircraft. Cadets learn airmanship both from books and hands-on training. Before they take a crack at

If an Air Force officer ever ends up in enemy territory, the evasion skills he or she learned from academy days will come in handy.

piloting a jet, cadets are trained in other forms of airmanship. Most cadets complete a sailplane program. About half will earn parachuting badges. Those cadets wishing to become pilots take an introductory course. But that's only the start of their work. Future pilots must make a ten-year training commitment to their dream.

Third degrees (sophomores) enroll in a Soar-for-All program. They begin the program by riding in the TG-7A motorglider. On the TG-7A, cadets become familiar with aircraft controls and checklists. As they gain experience, third degrees are allowed to spread their wings and prove their knowledge. Later in the year, they will begin to fly solo on sailplanes and aircraft such as the TG-4A. On TG-4A solo flights, cadets must pull off tricky maneuvers. For instance, they must make steep turns and recover from engine stalls.

Airmanship programs help teachers pick out which students will make good jet pilots. These programs also help to give cadets courage to jump out of an airplane. That's something you won't get at a civilian college!

CHARACTER COUNTS

Character is so important to the academy that there is even a Center for Character Development on school grounds. The center is based on the USAFA's core values: "Integrity first, Service before Self, Excellence in all we do." The center strives to make this motto mean something to cadets.

The Air Force Academy Honor Code is another important part of building a cadet's character. Each cadet makes this pledge: "We will not lie, steal or cheat, nor tolerate among us anyone who does." All cadets take formal courses in ethics. They also receive honor instruction as part of their military training.

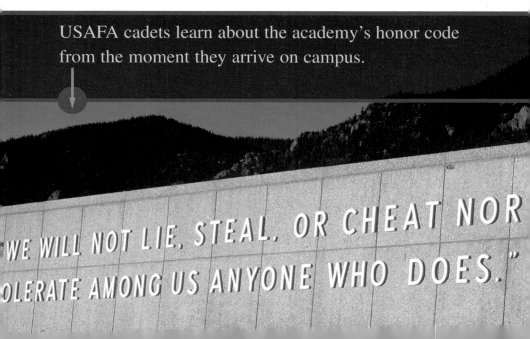

USAFA cadets learn about the academy's honor code from the moment they arrive on campus.

CHAPTER THREE

Beyond the Classroom

ATHLETICS

Athletics are an important part of USAFA curriculum. Each year, cadets take at least three different physical education courses. The USAFA's athletic program improves fitness. It also teaches physical skills and develops leadership qualities. The program encourages cadets to work as a team and bond together.

The academy fields teams in all the traditional sports including, baseball, wrestling, track, basketball, football, and soccer. The academy offers many intramural activities too. They include lacrosse, volleyball, fencing, gymnastics, and falconry. A campus fitness center provides a space to do cardiovascular training, such as running or aerobics. Other classes, such as yoga and Pilates, focus on combining physical and mental focus. Specialty classes in swimming and boxing are also available.

FALCONRY

The USAFA's mascot is a falcon. The falcon was chosen for its grace, power, and courage. Of course, this is also one fast bird. Falcons are known to fly at speeds of 200 miles per hour as they dive after prey. The academy's falcon mascot is nicknamed "Mach I." Mach I is the speed of sound— 760 miles per hour.

Falconry, or training birds of prey, is studied at the academy. Trained birds fly at major campus events, like football games. It takes months of training to prepare the birds for swooping among such huge crowds. The birds are taught to eat while perched on their trainer's fist. They learn how to respond to a shouted command and hit a lure. When the birds do something right, they're rewarded with small pieces of raw meat.

CLUBS AND LEISURE ACTIVITIES

If you're seeking a popular USAFA activity, look no further than the Aero Club. The Aero Club is for cadets who desire more personal flight training than the required courses provide. Those who join the Aero Club get an opportunity to fly Cessna 172s and T-41s. The Aero Club can train you in becoming a private or commercial pilot, or a flight instructor. The club also supports you in your instrument rating exam. Everyone who applies for a pilot's license must take this test.

The USAFA features a wide range of clubs. They include academic activities such as French and Spanish clubs. They also include artistic activities such as singing and playing an instrument. You could join the choir or march in the drum and bugle corps! If you have a knack for writing, join the staff of a campus magazine.

If your mind is taxed out, you can switch to a more physical option. Judo, karate, mountaineering, and even powerfishing clubs are offered on the academy grounds.

PARACHUTING

The most dramatic USAFA club may be the parachuting team, Wings of Blue. There is fierce competition to make this team. Those who do become part of a famous, elite group. Members must possess great courage. They also must have amazing body control to pull off such incredible turns, loops, and barrel rolls.

Each year, Wings of Blue delights crowds at major events like the Fiesta Bowl. At their demonstrations, a dozen Wings of Blue parachutists strut their stuff. They make four passes from different altitudes. The grand finale is the Bomb Burst Show. During this jump, four members form a four-man star at 11,000 feet. They break at 5,000 feet, and blue smoke trails from their bodies. They don't pull their ripcords until 2,500 feet—the last possible moment!

These daring moves aren't just acts of showing off. Freefall skills could come in handy during an emergency. If an aircraft becomes disabled, parachutists must know how to handle the situation calmly and skillfully.

BONDING

Only your fellow cadets know what it means to go through basic training. Only they are familiar with the parachute and pilot training that you've had. They, too, are studying the history and role of the military. These experiences give USAFA cadets a distinct outlook on life. Having these experiences in common with fellow cadets creates a special feeling of closeness. When you're in the wilderness—trying to scout for food and build a shelter—it's only natural to get close to the other cadets!

So now you know what your academy days will be like. But what happens once they end? What can you do with a Bachelor of Science degree? Must you complete military service after you've graduated? What military and civilian careers are available?

ACADEMY FACTS A few elite cadets are allowed to join the academy's sabre drill team. This team performs precise drills with three-foot-long, stainless steel swords. The drill sabre team appears at important ceremonies and sporting events. They also appear on the Miss USA Pageant, which is televised across the nation!

Firsties look forward to graduation ceremonies, which always send their spirits soaring.

CHAPTER FOUR

Taking Flight

After graduation, you will be ready to perform the duties of a U.S. Air Force officer. Graduates must fulfill a five-year military requirement. Your military requirement doesn't have to be served in the air force, though. You may apply for the army, navy, Marines Corps, or Coast Guard.

You can choose from several career paths: nontechnical, specialty, technical, or flight. Some graduates choose to go on to law or medical school. The military needs people in all sorts of professions.

Graduates who want to be pilots or navigators in the air force take a different path. They enter flight-training programs. It takes

Recent USAFA graduates can choose to serve in any of the five branches of the United States military.

about one year of flight-training instruction to earn your wings. Advanced instruction follows in flying fighter, bomber, or transport aircraft.

NONTECHNICAL CAREERS

It takes the talents of many people to keep the air force flying. Many air force jobs revolve around organizing or managing people and information. They range from air battle manager and communications commander to supply, intelligence, personnel, and transportation officers.

SPECIALITY CAREERS

You may choose to concentrate your skills in one specialized area. Here are some examples:

- Internists
- General practioners
- Medical commander
- Clinical psychologist
- Veterinary clinician
- Nurse-midwife
- Occupational therapist
- Physical therapist officer
- Allergists
- Pharmacists
- Social worker
- Dietitian officer
- Flight nurse
- Chaplain
- ...And many more!

USAFA graduates who wish to pilot or navigate aircraft receive intense flight training after completing

Military aircraft is highly complex. Without skilled cadets and officers helping run and fix bombers and jets, the USAF would remain grounded.

TECHNICAL CAREERS

Just think of all of the complicated equipment that is needed to keep the air force running. You could work with that equipment if you choose a technical career. You could design it, or make sure that it runs properly. The options for technical careers include engineering and aircraft maintenance. You could also become a munitions and missile maintenance officer, a scientist, or a civil engineer.

FLIGHT CAREERS

Do you want to survey foreign territory while flying reconnaissance missions? Do you picture yourself transporting equipment or dogfighting over the ocean? Maybe you always dreamed of becoming a pilot or navigator. Navigators are the people in the control towers who tell the pilots where it is safe to fly.

There are countless air force career paths that involve flying. You could pilot or navigate airlifts or bombers. Or maybe you would want to sit in the cockpit of an experimental aircraft. If you have a gift for teaching, you might make a fine pilot trainer. Another job might include manning the controls of a helicopter.

Air Apparent

There are certainly reasons to choose the USAFA over a traditional college. Of course, for many, a civilian university would be a better choice. Your decision depends on what you want your education to focus on. It also depends on whether you'd enjoy using your skills in the service of the military.

The USAFA has an excellent academic record. Many students win important academic scholarships. The academy has seen its share of Rhodes Scholars, as well as National Science Foundation and Guggenheim Fellows.

USAFA cadets face many challenges. But all the while, they learn important qualities of self-discipline, courage, leadership, and integrity. If you have the drive to push yourself to excellence, and want to make friends who are also driven, perhaps the USAFA is for you.

Spending four years at the USAFA is a demanding task. However, there are many graduates who are proud to say that they rose to the challenge.

NEW WORDS

airmanship the study of how to be a good pilot

assembly getting together in a group to hear important announcements

aviation the science and study of flying aircraft

cadet a student training to become an officer at a military service academy

civilian someone who is not in the military

curriculum a program of study for a school

ethics a set of moral beliefs

evasion the tactic of avoiding dangerous situations

NEW WORDS

extracurricular in addition to the regular schedule of classes

falconry training and caring for large birds of prey, especially hawks

integrity honor

majors fields of study on which you are focusing

mission statement a short description of what your plan and purpose is

navigate to get around

parachuting jumping out of an airplane using a parachute

FOR FURTHER READING

Ferrell, Nancy Warren. *The U. S. Air Force.* Minneapolis, MN: Lerner Publishing Group, 1990.

Hole, Dorothy. *The Air Force and You.* New York, NY: MacMilliam Publishing Company, 1993.

Langley, Wanda. *The Air Force in Action.* Berkeley Heights, NJ: Enslow Publishers, Incorporated, 2001.

Oberle, Lora Polack and Ellen Hopkins. *The Thunderbirds: The U. S. Air Force Aerial Demonstration Squadron.* Mankato, MN: Capstone Press, 2001.

RESOURCES

Web Sites

UNITED STATES AIR FORCE ACADEMY (USAFA) HOME PAGE

www.usafa.af.mil

USAFA ASSOCIATION OF GRADUATES

www.aog-usafa.org

RESOURCES

ORGANIZATION

HEADQUARTERS USAFA / RRS

2304 Cadet Drive, Suite 200
USAF Academy, CO 80840
(719) 333-2520

INDEX

INDEX

ABOUT THE AUTHOR

Magdalena Alagna is an editor and a freelance writer who lives in New York City.